It's in the File Folder!
Bible Games Series

Written by Mary J. Murray

Illustrated by Janet Armbrust

Cover Illustration by Janet Armbrust
Cover Production by Nehmen-Kodner

All rights reserved—Printed in the U.S.A.
Copyright © 2001 Shining Star Publications
A Division of Frank Schaffer Publications, Inc.
23740 Hawthorne Blvd., Torrance, CA 90505

Notice! Pages may be reproduced for home or classroom use only, not for commercial resale. No part of this publication may be reproduced for storage in a retrieval system, or transmitted in any form or by any means—electronic, mechanical, recording, etc.—without the prior written permission of the publisher. Reproduction of these materials for an entire school or school system is strictly prohibited.

Unless otherwise indicated, the New International Version of the Bible was used in preparing the activities in this book. Scripture taken from the HOLY BIBLE, NEW INTERNATIONAL VERSION. Copyright © 1973, 1978, 1984 International Bible Society. Used by permission of Zondervan Bible Publishers.

Introduction

This book contains everything you need to make fourteen Bible-based learning games for children in grades K–3. Young children will delight in these fun and exciting games that make God's Word come alive.

These games are ideal for use in the Sunday school or Christian school classroom or at home. Each game is based on a passage of Scripture that is relevant and applicable to a young child's life. Be sure to encourage discussion about the theme of each game so that the children come to understand how God's Word directly affects their lives.

Each game can be easily assembled and then stored in a file folder and a 2-quart resealable plastic bag. Directions are clearly stated and easy to follow. The materials required for each game are readily available and inexpensive.

On page 4, you will find a recording page depicting all fourteen file folder games. Children can use this page to help them keep track of which games they have played. Encourage them to color in each numbered file folder picture as they play the corresponding game.

Organizing the Games

If you are a classroom teacher, you may want to ask for parent volunteers or older students (perhaps a youth group) to help assemble each file folder game. (It is recommended that you laminate the prepared file folder, mount the playing pieces on tagboard, and then laminate them for durability.) After assembling all the games, print a number between 1 and 14 on the outside of each file folder, as shown on the recording page. Store the folders in a box or crate so that they are easily accessible to the children. Pairs or small groups of children can play the games independently after they have completed other class work.

You might also allow each child to "make and take" a game from time to time. In this case, reproduce the pages from the book and allow each child to prepare his or her own game to keep. Families will enjoy working together to assemble and play each game.

If you are using these games in a home setting, let your child help assemble and construct each game. Children learn and develop a variety of skills by participating in the preparation.

Each game includes the following components:

- featured Bible verse card—Make a copy of this verse card for the children whenever a new game is introduced to help the children enhance Scripture memory. A copy of it is also mounted on the file folder.

- materials needed list

- directions for assembling the file folder game

- 4 reproducible labels—1. a game label; 2. a directions card (how to play); 3. an Extra Fun! card (a suggested activity designed to enhance children's understanding of the game's concept); 4. a file folder tab label

- one or more pages of patterns to be mounted in the file folder or used with the game

Also included at the back of the book is a Reflections page. The children can use this page to share their opinions about their favorite game and Scripture.

You and your children are sure to enjoy learning about and discussing God's Word as you also have some hands-on fun together with *It's in the File Folder*.

Table of Contents

Recording Page 4
Good Works (Ephesians 2:10) 5–9
Think About These Things (Philippians 4:8) 10–14
Be Fruitful (Galatians 5:22–23) 15–18
Bee-Attitudes (Matthew 5:1–2) 19–22
Down by the Sea (Genesis 1:21) 23–27
Ready to Run (Hebrews 12:1) 28–31
Just Like Deer (Psalm 42:1) 32–36
Eat and Drink (1 Corinthians 10:31) 37–40
Food and Clothing (1 Timothy 6:8) 41–44
Counting on God (Exodus 11:1 and John 6:11) 45–48
A Place for You (John 14:3) 49–52
Joseph (Genesis 50:20) 53–56
He Is the Vine (John 15:5) 57–59
The Birds of the Air (Genesis 1:21) 60–63
Reflections Page 64

Recording Page

Name _____

Good Works

God wants us to show our love for Him by doing good things for the people in our lives. This includes loving, helping, and giving to the people we live with, work with, and play with. It also includes people we don't even know. By doing "good works," we are bringing God glory, and that gives Him great pleasure! Children will be encouraged to do "good works" for others and bring glory to God as they play this matching game.

Materials Needed

1 copy of the Bible verse card below; 1 copy of the labels and cards on page 6; 1 copy of the children on pages 8–9; 1 copy of the T–shirts and number cards on page 7; manila file folder; 2-quart resealable plastic freezer bag; clothespin; scissors; crayons; glue; tagboard

Directions

1. Color, cut out, and mount the game label on the front of the file folder.
2. Color, cut out, and mount the file folder tab on the tab of the file folder.
3. Cut out and mount the Bible verse card on the top left-hand side of the inside of the folder.
4. Cut out the directions card and extra fun card. Mount them on tagboard and place them inside the plastic bag.
5. Color and cut out the faces. Mount them on the inside of the file folder.
6. Color each T-shirt to match one of the hats on the faces.
7. Mount page 7 on tagboard. Cut out the T-shirts and number cards and store them in the plastic bag.
8. Clip the bag to the folder with the clothespin or drop it inside the file folder.
9. Model how to play the game from start to finish.

Bible Verse Card

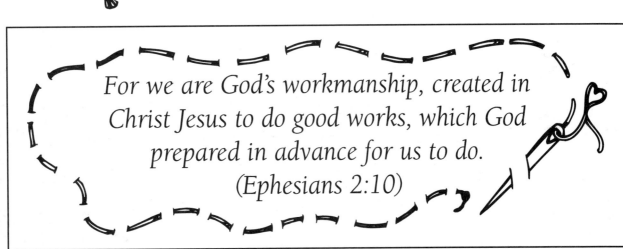

For we are God's workmanship, created in Christ Jesus to do good works, which God prepared in advance for us to do.
(Ephesians 2:10)

Game Label

Good Works

Extra Fun!

Work together to write a list of "good works" that you can do, or write a list of people for whom you can do "good works."

Directions Card

Good Works

Number of Players: 1 or 2

How to Play:

1. Lay the number cards facedown on the table.
2. Lay the T-shirts faceup on the table.
3. Read the Bible verse aloud.
4. Decide who will go first.
5. Player One turns over a number card, finds the matching number on the game board, and identifies the pattern on the hat (stripes, hearts, polka-dots, etc.).
6. Player One then finds the matching T-shirt, reads aloud the "good work" written on it, and matches the T-shirt to the hat on the game board.
7. Continue taking turns until all the numbers have been drawn.
8. At the end of the game, add up the sum of your number cards. See who has the highest number.

File Folder Tab

Good Works

T-Shirts and Number Cards

Faces

Faces

Think About These Things

God's Word is very clear about what we should and should not think about. God wants our minds to be on Him and on things above. (Matthew 22:37; Colossians 3:2) This game will encourage young believers to think about things that are excellent and worthy of praise, as Paul talks about in Philippians 4:8.

Materials Needed

- 1 copy of the Bible verse card below
- 1 copy of the labels and cards on page 11
- 1 copy of the game board pieces on pages 12 and 13
- 1 copy of the word cards on page 14
- manila file folder
- 2-quart resealable plastic freezer bag
- clothespin
- scissors
- crayons
- glue
- tagboard

Directions

1. Color, cut out, and mount the game label on the front of the file folder.
2. Color, cut out, and mount the file folder tab on the tab of the file folder.
3. Cut out and mount the Bible verse card on the top left-hand side of the inside of the folder.
4. Cut out the directions card and extra fun card. Mount them on tagboard and place them inside the plastic bag.
5. Color and cut out the game board pieces. Mount them on the inside of the file folder.
6. Mount the word cards on tagboard, cut them out, and store them in the plastic bag.
7. Clip the bag to the folder with the clothespin, or drop it inside the file folder.
8. Model how to play the game from start to finish.

Finally, brothers, whatever is true, whatever is noble, whatever is right, whatever is pure, whatever is lovely, whatever is admirable—if anything is excellent or praiseworthy—think about such things.
(Philippians 4:8)

Bible Verse Card

© Shining Star Publications SS20018

10

Game Label

Think About These Things

Extra Fun!

Extra Fun!

Draw a picture of your face on the bottom half of a sheet of drawing paper. Make an idea bubble above your head. Inside the bubble, draw pictures or write words of things you can think about that would be pleasing to God.

Directions Card

Think About These Things

Number of Players: 2

How to Play:
1. Read the Bible verse aloud.
2. Match each word card to the dialogue bubble on the game board.
3. As you read each word card aloud, name something that is lovely, pure, right, etc.

File Folder Tab

Think About These Things

Game Board Pieces

Game Board Pieces

Word Cards

- noble
- lovely
- pure
- admirable
- true
- praiseworthy
- right
- excellent

Be Fruitful

God's Word lists the fruits of the Spirit that should show in our lives when we believe in Him and allow His Word to change us. If we see the fruits of God's love in our lives, we know that we are growing to become more like His Son, the Lord Jesus Christ. Children will learn and grow as they match these colorful fruit pieces and then read a Scripture verse related to each fruit of the Spirit.

Materials Needed

- 1 copy of the Bible verse card below
- 1 copy of the labels and cards on page 16
- 2 copies of the numbered fruit frame on page 17
- 2 copies of the fruit word cards on page 18
- manila file folder
- 2-quart resealable plastic freezer bag
- clothespin
- scissors
- crayons
- glue
- tagboard
- 2 dice

Directions

1. Color, cut out, and mount the game label on the front of the file folder.
2. Color, cut out, and mount the file folder tab on the tab of the file folder.
3. Cut out and mount the Bible verse card on the top left-hand side of the inside of the folder.
4. Cut out the directions card and extra fun card. Mount them on tagboard and place them inside the plastic bag.
5. Color the two numbered fruit frames and mount them on the inside of the file folder.
6. Color both copies of the fruit word cards, mount them on tagboard, cut them out, and store them in the plastic bag.
7. Place the dice inside the plastic bag.
8. Clip the bag to the folder with the clothespin, or drop it inside the file folder.
9. Model how to play the game from start to finish.

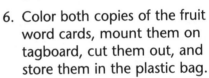

Bible Verse Card

But the fruit of the Spirit is love, joy, peace, patience, kindness, goodness, faithfulness, gentleness and self-control . . .
(Galatians 5:22–23)

Game Label

Be Fruitful

Extra Fun!

Choose one Bible verse from the game board. Cut that shape of fruit from a piece of construction paper. Print the Bible verse in large bold letters on the paper fruit. Hang the fruit piece in your home as a reminder to practice being fruitful.

Directions Card

Be Fruitful

Number of Players: 2

How to Play:

1. Read the Bible verse aloud.
2. Lay both sets of fruit word cards in order across the table, according to Galatians 5:22–23.
3. Decide who will go first.
4. Player One rolls the dice and then adds or subtracts the numbers on the dice to equal a numbered fruit on his or her side of the game board.
5. Player One reads the verse from that fruit, then covers it with a matching fruit word card.
6. If Player One cannot add or subtract the numbers on the dice to equal one of his or her numbers, Player One passes.
7. Continue the game until both players have covered all of their numbered fruit.

File Folder Tab

Be Fruitful

© Shining Star Publications SS20018

Numbered Fruit Frame

Fruit Word Cards

- goodness
- patience
- gentleness
- joy
- faithfulness
- self-control
- love
- kindness
- peace

Bee-Attitudes

Jesus begins His teaching of the Sermon on the Mount with the beatitudes. In this well-known passage of Scripture, Jesus instructs His disciples to be merciful, righteous, peaceable, and pure in heart. In essence, He's teaching them to become like He is. He wants us to learn the same thing. Jesus also tells of the great blessings we will receive when we live by these principles. Children will enjoy playing this matching game as they learn more about the teachings of Jesus.

Materials Needed

- 1 copy of the Bible verse card below
- 1 copy of the labels and cards on page 20
- 1 copy of the beehives and Scripture card on page 21
- 1 copy of the bees on page 22
- manila file folder
- 2-quart resealable plastic freezer bag
- clothespin
- scissors
- crayons
- glue
- tagboard

Directions

1. Color, cut out, and mount the game label on the front of the file folder.
2. Color, cut out, and mount the file folder tab on the tab of the file folder.
3. Cut out and mount the Bible verse card on the top left-hand side of the inside of the folder.
4. Cut out the directions card and extra fun card. Mount them on tagboard and place them inside the plastic bag.
5. Color and cut out the beehives. Mount them on the inside of the file folder as shown.
6. Color the bees and Scripture card, mount them on tagboard, and store them in the plastic bag.
7. Clip the bag to the folder with the clothespin, or drop it inside the file folder.
8. Model how to play the game from start to finish.

Bible Verse Card

Now when he saw the crowds, he went up on a mountainside and sat down. His disciples came to him, and he began to teach them . . .
(Matthew 5:1–2)

Game Label

Bee-Attitudes

Extra Fun!

Extra Fun!

Draw several bees around the border of a sheet of paper. Inside the border, draw a picture or write about Jesus teaching you to be merciful, pure in heart, righteous, a peacemaker, etc.

Directions Card

Bee-Attitudes

Number of Players: 2

How to Play:

1. Read the Bible verse aloud.
2. Read a Scripture verse from one of the beehives on the game board.
3. Look for the bee that contains the Scripture to complete that Scripture verse. (You can refer to the Scripture card for help.)
4. Place each bee near its matching beehive.

File Folder Tab

Bee-Attitudes

© Shining Star Publications SS20018

Beehives

- "Blessed are the poor in spirit . . ."
- "Blessed are those who mourn . . ."
- "Blessed are the meek . . ."
- "Blessed are those who hunger and thirst for righteousness . . ."
- "Blessed are the merciful . . ."
- "Blessed are the pure in heart . . ."
- "Blessed are the peacemakers . . ."
- "Blessed are those who are persecuted because of righteousness . . ."

Scripture Card

Matthew 5:3–10

3. "Blessed are the poor in spirit, for theirs is the kingdom of heaven."

4. "Blessed are those who mourn, for they will be comforted."

5. "Blessed are the meek, for they will inherit the earth."

6. "Blessed are those who hunger and thirst for righteousness, for they will be filled."

7. "Blessed are the merciful, for they will be shown mercy."

8. "Blessed are the pure in heart, for they will see God."

9. "Blessed are the peacemakers, for they will be called sons of God."

10. "Blessed are those who are persecuted because of righteousness, for theirs is the kingdom of heaven."

Bees

"... for theirs is the kingdom of heaven."

"... for they will be called sons of God."

"... for they will be shown mercy."

"... for they will see God."

"... for they will inherit the earth."

"... for they will be filled."

"... for theirs is the kingdom of heaven."

"... for they will be comforted."

Down by the Sea

On the fifth day of creation, God created all the great creatures of the sea. (Genesis 1:21) We are reminded of God's great power when we think about the ocean and remember that The sea is his, for he made it . . . (Psalm 95:5) You will enjoy watching the children's excitement as they practice reading and spelling the names of some of these great sea creatures and move across the ocean floor on this colorful game board.

Materials Needed

- 1 copy of the Bible verse card below
- 1 copy of the labels and cards on page 24
- 1 copy of the sea game board on pages 26 and 27
- 2 copies of the word cards on page 25
- manila file folder
- 2-quart resealable plastic freezer bag
- clothespin
- scissors
- crayons
- glue
- tagboard
- 4 different, small seashells (game markers)

Directions

1. Color, cut out, and mount the game label on the front of the file folder.
2. Color, cut out, and mount the file folder tab on the tab of the file folder.
3. Cut out the directions card and extra fun card. Mount them on tagboard, and place them inside the plastic bag.
4. Color and cut out the game board. Mount it on the inside of the file folder as shown.
5. Cut out and mount the Bible verse card on the top left-hand side of the inside of the folder.
6. Color the pictures on the word cards, mount them on tagboard, cut them apart, and store them in the plastic bag.
7. Place the seashells inside the plastic bag.
8. Clip the bag to the folder with the clothespin or drop it inside the file folder.
9. Model how to play the game from start to finish.

Bible Verse Card

So God created the great creatures of the sea and every living and moving thing with which the water teems, according to their kinds . . . And God saw that it was good.
(Genesis 1:21)

Game Label

Down by the Sea

Extra Fun!

Use construction paper, scissors, glue, crayons, and other available materials to make an ocean scene. Include some of the ocean animals mentioned in the game. Print the verse from Genesis 1:21 across the top of the page.

Directions Card

Down by the Sea

Number of Players: 2–4

How to Play:
1. Stack the word cards facedown.
2. Choose a seashell as your game marker.
3. Set your markers at the starting line.
4. Read the Bible verse aloud.
5. Decide who will go first.
6. The person sitting to the left of Player One draws a word card and reads it aloud.
7. Player One is asked to name the beginning letter of the word and spell the word(s)*. If Player One identifies the beginning letter correctly, he or she moves ahead one space. If Player One spells the word correctly, he or she moves ahead two more spaces.
8. Continue the game until all players reach the end of the game board.
9. Shuffle and restack the word cards if necessary.

*Have younger children name the ending letter or sound instead of spelling each word.

File Folder Tab

Down by the Sea

© Shining Star Publications   SS20018

24

Word Cards

sperm whale	lobster	sea anemone
shark	clam	shrimp
sea horse	dolphin	squid
blue whale	tuna	eel
jellyfish	octopus	lionfish
starfish	angelfish	crab

Game Board

Game Board

Ready to Run

Living the Christian life is often compared to running a race. As believers, we need to train ourselves in righteousness, always persevere, and keep our eyes fixed on the finish line (eternity in heaven with God). In order to live a life that is pleasing to God and run the race for Him, we also need to throw off the things that will slow us down. Hebrews 12:1 tells us to throw off the sin that entangles us so that we can run the race well. You will enjoy seeing the children share their ideas about throwing off specific sins as they play this game together.

Materials Needed

- 1 copy of the Bible verse card below
- 1 copy of the labels and cards on page 29
- 1 copy of the runners on page 30
- 1 copy of the puzzle pieces on page 31
- manila file folder
- 2-quart resealable plastic freezer bag
- clothespin
- scissors
- crayons
- glue
- tagboard
- coin

Directions

1. Color, cut out, and mount the game label on the front of the file folder.
2. Color, cut out, and mount the file folder tab on the tab of the file folder.
3. Cut out and mount the Bible verse card on the top left-hand side of the inside of the folder.
4. Cut out the directions card and extra fun card. Mount them on tagboard and place them inside the plastic bag.
5. Color and cut out the runners. Mount them on the inside of the file folder as shown.
6. Mount the puzzle pieces on tagboard, cut them apart, and store them in the plastic bag.
7. Place the coin inside the plastic bag.
8. Clip the bag to the folder with the clothespin or drop it inside the file folder.
9. Model how to play the game from start to finish.

. . . let us throw off everything that hinders and the sin that so easily entangles, and let us run with perseverance the race marked out for us. (Hebrews 12:1)

Bible Verse Card

Game Label

Ready to Run

Extra Fun!

Extra Fun!

Trace your footprint onto construction paper. Cut out the shape. Print the verse from Hebrews 12:1 on the footprint. Decorate the footprint with crayons or markers.

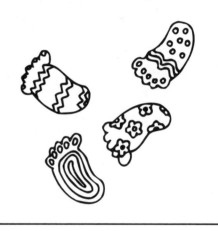

Directions Card

Ready to Run

Number of Players: 2

How to Play:

1. Divide the puzzle pieces into two piles (dark, light). Give each pile to a player.
2. Each player chooses a runner.
3. Cover your runner with one set of the puzzle pieces, placing them in order from 1 to 12.
4. Read the Bible verse aloud.
5. Decide who will go first.
6. Player One tosses the coin and removes one or two puzzle pieces from his or her runner. *Heads: Remove two puzzle pieces; *Tails: Remove one puzzle piece. (Players lose a turn if the correct amount of puzzle pieces cannot be removed.)
7. Read each word aloud as you remove that puzzle piece. Give an example of what it will look like to remove that sin from your life. (Example: Anger—I won't get angry if my sister plays with my toys.)
8. Take turns until one runner is ready for the race and has "thrown off all his or her sin."

*Note: Three words are written on two puzzle pieces. These pairs of puzzle pieces must be removed at the same time.

File Folder Tab

Ready to Run

Runners

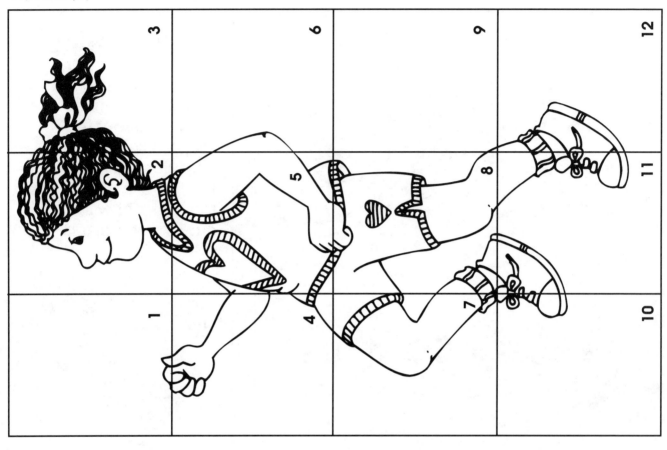

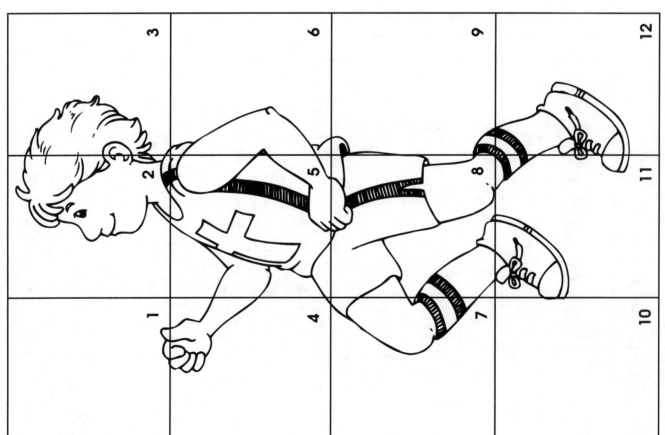

Puzzle Pieces

arguing 1	worry 2	f e a r 3	
hate 4	selfish ness 5	6	
complaining 7	complaining 8	lying 9	
anger 10	disobe dience 11	disobe dience 12	

Just Like Deer

In Psalm 42, the psalmist compares his soul longing for God to a deer panting for water. God wants us to desire Him, thirst for Him, and long for Him, too. You'll enjoy watching the children explore God's Word as their souls thirst for Him through a fresh look at the Scripture.

Materials Needed

1 copy of the Bible verse card below
1 copy of the labels and cards on page 33
1 copy of the game board on pages 34 and 35
1 copy of the deer verse cards on page 36
manila file folder
2-quart resealable plastic freezer bag
clothespin
scissors
crayons
glue
tagboard
Bible

Directions

1. Color, cut out, and mount the game label on the front of the file folder.
2. Color, cut out, and mount the file folder tab on the tab of the file folder.
3. Cut out the directions card and extra fun card. Mount them on tagboard and place them inside the plastic bag.
4. Color and cut out the game board. Mount it on the inside of the file folder as shown.
5. Cut out and mount the Bible verse card on the top left-hand side of the inside of the folder.
6. Color the deer, mount the page on tagboard, and cut out the deer. (For younger children, you may want to write one of the Bible references listed below on each deer.)
7. Clip the bag to the folder with the clothespin or drop it inside the file folder.
8. Model how to play the game from start to finish.

1. Psalm 27:8	3. Psalm 63:5	5. Psalm 119:35	7. Psalm 63:1	9. Psalm 95:6
2. Psalm 62:1	4. Psalm 119:72	6. Psalm 42:1	8. Psalm 118:28	10. Psalm 103:1

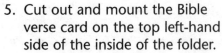

As the deer pants for streams of water, so my soul pants for you, O God. (Psalm 42:1)

Game Label

Just Like Deer

Extra Fun!

Extra Fun!

Write a prayer to God telling Him how much you love Him and how your soul thirsts for Him. Draw a picture of a deer on the page to remind you of Psalm 42. Pray the prayer and read Psalm 42 each day for one week.

Directions Card

Just Like Deer

Number of Players: 1 or 2

How to Play:

1. Read the Bible verse aloud.
2. Stack the deer cards facedown on the table.
3. Turn over the top card and read the verse aloud.
4. Match the deer to the Bible reference on the pond. (Older children will need to look up each reference listed by the pond and then match each deer to its reference.)
5. Continue until all the deer are at the pond.

File Folder Tab

Just Like Deer

Game Board

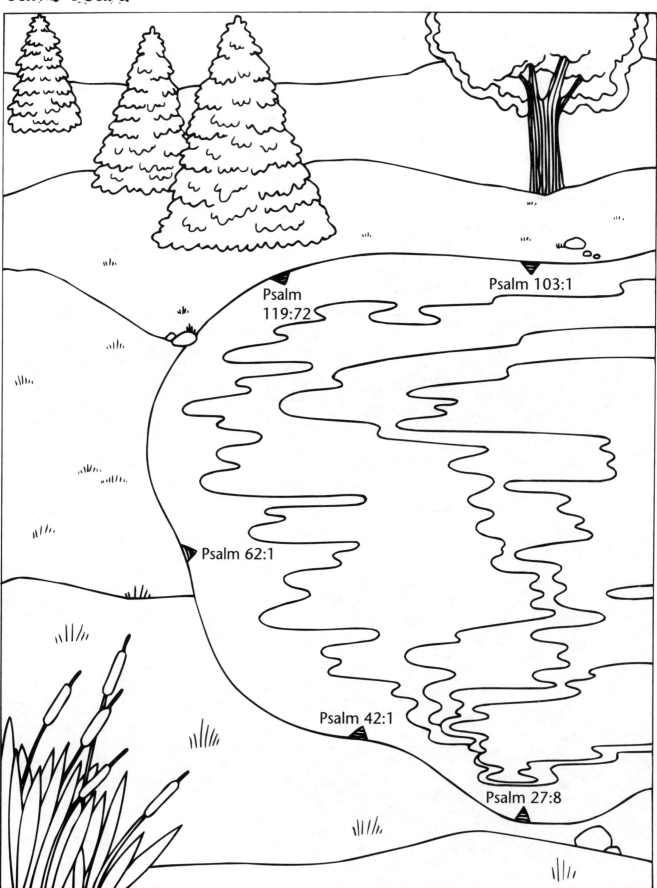

Deer Verse Cards

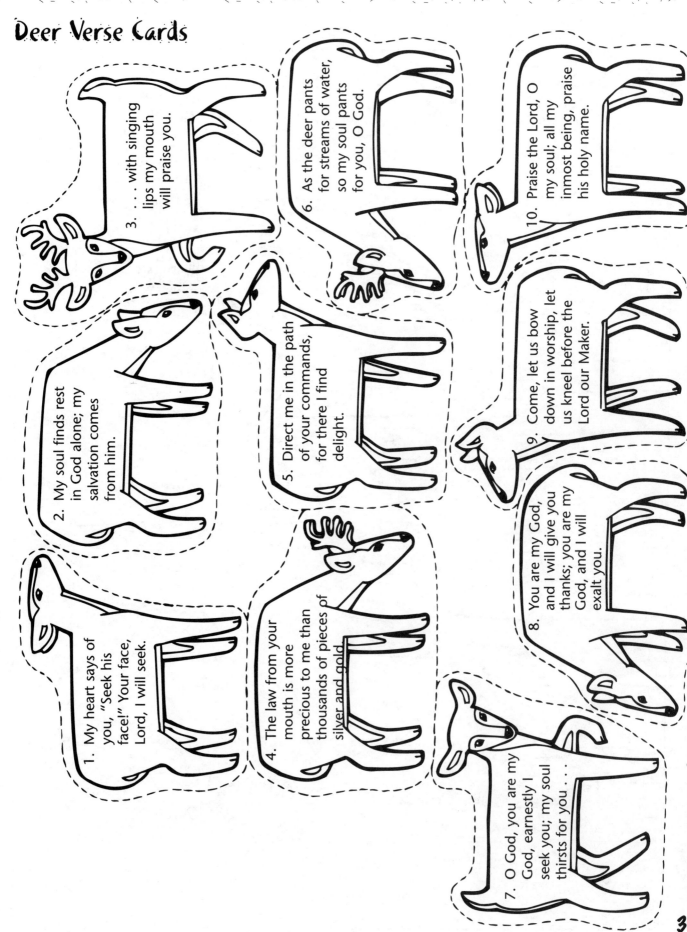

Eat and Drink

1 Corinthians 10:31 says that whether we eat or drink, we are to do it all for the glory of God. God wants us to thankfully enjoy the abundance of foods and beverages with which He has lovingly provided us. And He wants us to think of Him in everything we do, even when we eat and drink. Young believers will be encouraged to eat and drink for God's glory as they play this food sorting game.

Materials Needed

- 1 copy of the Bible verse card below
- 1 copy of the labels and cards on page 38
- 1 copy of the picture cards, labels, and letter cards on pages 39 and 40
- manila file folder
- 2-quart resealable plastic freezer bag
- clothespin
- scissors
- crayons
- glue
- tagboard
- small envelope
- *optional: plastic or magnetic letters

Directions

1. Color, cut out, and mount the game label on the front of the file folder.
2. Color, cut out, and mount the file folder tab on the tab of the file folder.
3. Cut out and mount the Bible verse card on the top left-hand side of the inside of the folder.
4. Cut out the directions card and extra fun card. Mount them on tagboard and place them inside the plastic bag.
5. Color and cut out the EAT and DRINK labels. Mount them on the inside of the file folder as shown.
6. Color the picture cards, mount them on tagboard, cut them out, and store them in the plastic bag.
7. Cut out the letters and place them in the envelope (or use the plastic letters).
8. Place the envelope in the plastic bag.
9. Clip the bag to the folder with the clothespin or drop it inside the file folder.
10. Model how to play the game from start to finish.

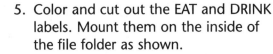

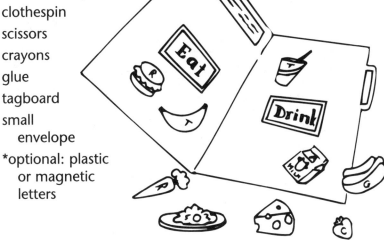

So whether you eat or drink or whatever you do, do it all for the glory of God.
(1 Corinthians 10:31)

Game Label

Eat and Drink

Extra Fun!

Extra Fun!

Cut pictures of food and drinks from magazines. Paste them in collage formation on a piece of construction paper. Cut 23 one-inch squares from another color of construction paper. Print one letter on each square, spelling out "*Do it all for the glory of God.*" Glue the letters in order across the top of the page. Share the Bible verse with a friend or family member.

Directions Card

Eat and Drink

Number of Players: 2

How to Play:

1. Read the Bible verse aloud.
2. Sort the picture cards into two groups on the folder (eat/drink).
3. Place a matching letter card on top of each picture card.
4. Remove the letters from the picture cards. Use them to spell out the phrase, *Do it all for the glory of God.*
5. Talk about ways people can eat and drink to honor God. Talk about ways people eat and drink that do not honor God.

File Folder Tab

Eat and Drink

© Shining Star Publications
SS20018

Labels

Eat

Drink

Picture Cards

Letter Cards

D	O	I	T	A	L	L	F
O	R	T	H	E	G	L	O
R	Y	O	F	G	O	D	(1 Corinthians 10:31)

Picture Cards

Food and Clothing

The Bible teaches us to be content with food and clothing. (1 Timothy 6:8) The apostle Paul was an excellent example for us to follow. He suffered in many ways and yet was able to say "I have learned to be content in any situation." (Philippians 4:12) In today's world, we are often tempted to want more, bigger, and better things. Young believers will be reminded to be content with food and clothing as they play this game.

Materials Needed

- 1 copy of the Bible verse card below
- 1 copy of the labels and cards on page 42
- 1 copy of the game board on page 43
- 1 copy per child of the recording page (page 44)
- manila file folder
- 2-quart resealable plastic freezer bag
- clothespin
- scissors
- crayons
- glue
- tagboard
- large paper clip
- 8 crayons—basic colors
- pencil
- die

Directions

1. Color, cut out, and mount the game label on the front of the file folder.
2. Color, cut out, and mount the file folder tab on the tab of the file folder.
3. Cut out and mount the Bible verse card on the top left-hand side of the inside of the folder.
4. Cut out the directions card and extra fun card. Mount them on tagboard and place them inside the plastic bag.
5. Color and cut out the game board. Mount it on the right side of the inside of the file folder as shown.
6. Clip several copies of the blank recording page to the left side of the inside of the folder.
7. Place the crayons, pencil, game markers, and die inside the plastic bag.
8. Clip the bag to the folder with the clothespin or drop it inside the file folder.
9. Model how to play the game from start to finish.

Bible Verse Card

But if we have food and clothing, we will be content with that.
(1 Timothy 6:8)

Game Label

Food and Clothing

Extra Fun!

Extra Fun!

Fold a sheet of paper in half. On the top half of the page, draw three things you wish you could have. On the bottom half of the page, draw 10 things you already have. On the back of the paper, write a short prayer to God thanking Him for all that He has given you. Ask Him to help you learn to be content with what you have.

Directions Card

Food and Clothing

Number of Players: 2

How to Play:

1. Read the Bible verse aloud.
2. Each player takes a recording page and sets his or her marker on Start.
3. Players take turns rolling the die and moving their markers around the game board.
4. As each player lands on a space, he or she uses crayons to draw the item pictured on the recording page. Once drawn, the player then checks it off at the bottom of the page.
5. The goal is to see who gets all seven food and clothing items drawn first.
6. If a player lands on an item he or she doesn't need, the player passes.

File Folder Tab

Food and Clothing

Game Board

Food and Clothing Recording Page

Counting on God

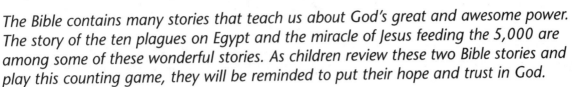 

The Bible contains many stories that teach us about God's great and awesome power. The story of the ten plagues on Egypt and the miracle of Jesus feeding the 5,000 are among some of these wonderful stories. As children review these two Bible stories and play this counting game, they will be reminded to put their hope and trust in God.

Materials Needed

- 1 copy of the Bible verse cards below
- 1 copy of the labels and cards on page 46
- 1 copy of the story and number cards on pages 47 and 48
- manila file folder
- 2-quart resealable plastic freezer bag
- clothespin
- scissors
- crayons
- glue
- tagboard
- 20 dry beans
- resealable sandwich bag
- *optional: 20 one-inch square tiles, (two sets of ten tiles, numbered 1–10)

Directions

1. Color, cut out, and mount the game label on the front of the file folder.
2. Color, cut out, and mount the file folder tab label on the tab of the file folder.
3. Cut out and mount each Bible verse card inside the folder as shown.
4. Cut out the directions card and extra fun card. Mount them on tagboard and place them inside the plastic bag.
5. Color and cut out the story cards. Mount them inside the file folder beneath the Bible verses.
6. Color the number cards and mount them on tagboard.
7. Cut out the number cards and store them in the plastic bag.
8. Place the dry beans in the sandwich bag and place it inside the plastic bag.
9. Clip the bag to the folder with the clothespin or drop it inside the file folder.
10. Model how to play the game from start to finish.

Bible Verse Cards

 Jesus then took the loaves, gave thanks, and distributed to those who were seated as much as they wanted. He did the same with the fish. (John 6:11)

 Now the Lord had said to Moses, "I will bring one more plague on Pharaoh and on Egypt . . ." (Exodus 11:1)

Game Label

Counting on God

Extra Fun!

Extra Fun!

Choose one of your favorite Bible stories and make a story card like the ones in this game. Draw a scene from that Bible story. Include groups of items between 1 and 10. Cut ten 1-inch squares from paper. Print a number between 1 and 10 on each square. Draw a small picture of one item in each of the 10 groups you drew. Have a friend complete the counting activity.

Directions Card

Counting on God

Number of Players: 1 or 2

How to Play:

1. Read the Bible verses aloud.
2. Choose a story card.
3. Find and count how many of each item is in the picture.
4. Place the matching number card in the correct space at the bottom of the page.
5. If necessary, use the beans to keep track of the items you count.
6. Continue until you've counted all the items on each story card.

File Folder Tab

Counting on God

Number Cards

1
2
3
4
5
6
7
8
9
10

Story Card

Story Card

Number Cards

48

A Place for You

In the book of John, Jesus promises to prepare a place for each of us in heaven with Him. This is a wonderful promise for all of us who believe in Jesus as our Savior and God! This game will encourage children to look forward to reaching heaven and will offer them good reminders for obedience along the way.

Materials Needed

- 1 copy of the Bible verse card below
- 1 copy of the labels and cards on page 50
- 1 copy of the game board and spinner on pages 51 and 52
- manila file folder
- 2-quart resealable plastic freezer bag
- clothespin
- scissors
- crayons
- glue
- tagboard
- paper clip
- paper fastener
- 4 game markers

Directions

1. Color, cut out, and mount the game label on the front of the file folder.
2. Color, cut out, and mount the file folder tab on the tab of the file folder.
3. Cut out and mount the Bible verse card on the top left-hand side of the inside of the folder.
4. Cut out the directions card and extra fun card. Mount them on tagboard and place them inside the plastic bag.
5. Color and cut out the game board. Mount it on the inside of the file folder.
6. Color the spinner, and mount it on tagboard. Put a paper clip on the center of the spinner. Attach the spinner and paper clip to the game board by inserting the paper fastener through the file folder. Be sure the spinner spins freely.
7. Place the markers inside the plastic bag.
8. Clip the bag to the folder with the clothespin or drop it inside the file folder.
9. Model how to play the game from start to finish.

"And if I go and prepare a place for you, I will come back and take you to be with me that you also may be where I am." (John 14:3)

Game Label

A Place for You

Extra Fun!

Extra Fun!

Use colored chalk on construction paper (or other art supplies) to draw a picture of what you think heaven will be like. Write about heaven on another sheet of paper. Then attach it to your drawing.

Directions Card

A Place for You

Number of Players: 2

How to Play:

1. Read the Bible verse aloud.
2. Decide who will go first.
3. Set your markers on Start.
4. Take turns spinning the spinner and moving along the game board the correct number of spaces.
5. If a player lands on a space with an arrow, he or she follows the arrow and gives an example of how to do what is written on that space or how to avoid doing it (sin).
6. Play until everyone gets to heaven.

File Folder Tab

A Place for You

Game Board

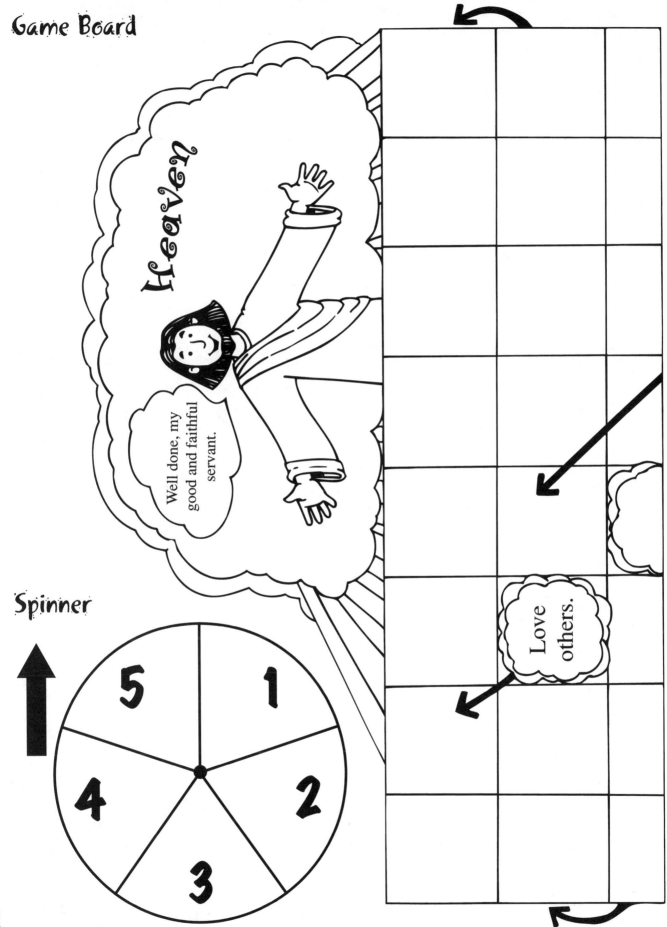

Heaven

Well done, my good and faithful servant.

Love others.

Spinner

START

Read the Bible.

SIN

Serve God.

SIN

Trust in the Lord.

Keep your eyes fixed on Jesus.

Love the Lord your God.

© Shining Star Publications SS20018

Joseph

The story of Joseph (Genesis 37–50) shows us how God can use any situation or circumstance and make it work for good. Joseph was his father's favorite son. This made his brothers very jealous. Joseph's brothers intended to harm him, but God intended for this to happen as it would help Him accomplish His purpose. (Genesis 50:19) Young believers will enjoy reviewing Joseph's life as they move along the game board and put together the pieces of Joseph's coat of many colors.

Materials Needed

- 1 copy of the Bible verse card below
- 1 copy of the labels and cards on page 54
- 1 copy of the game board and puzzle pieces on pages 55 and 56
- manila file folder
- 2-quart resealable plastic freezer bag
- clothespin
- scissors
- crayons
- glue
- tagboard
- 2 markers
- die
- *Optional: children's picture Bible

Directions

1. Color, cut out, and mount the game label on the front of the file folder.
2. Color, cut out, and mount the file folder tab on the tab of the file folder.
3. Cut out and mount the Bible verse card on the top left-hand side of the inside of the folder.
4. Cut out the directions card and extra fun card. Mount them on tagboard, and place them inside the plastic bag.
5. Color the game board and cut it out along the dotted lines. Mount the pages on the inside of the file folder.
6. Color the coat puzzle pieces, mount them on tagboard, and cut them apart on the solid lines.
7. Place the coat puzzle pieces, the die, and the markers in the plastic bag.
8. Clip the bag to the folder with the clothespin or drop it inside the file folder.

*You can use a children's picture Bible to review the story of Joseph. Then model how to play the game from start to finish.

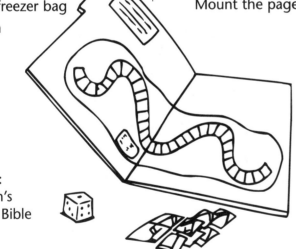

Bible Verse Card

"... God intended it for good to accomplish what is now being done ..." (Genesis 50:20)

Game Label

Joseph

Extra Fun!

Extra Fun!

Design a colorful coat of your own. Draw the shape of a coat on a piece of construction paper. Cut it out. Use crayons, construction paper scraps, scissors, and glue to decorate the coat. Print the key verse, Genesis 50:20, on the back of the coat. Hang it in your home to remind you that God worked things out for good in Joseph's life, and He's also working in yours.

Directions Card

Joseph

Number of Players: 2

How to Play:
1. Read the Bible verse aloud.
2. Set your markers on Start.
3. Player One rolls the die and moves the correct number of spaces.
4. Players must refer to the key at the bottom of the game board for special instructions.
5. The first player to complete the coat puzzle and reach the end of the game board is the winner.

File Folder Tab

Joseph

© Shining Star Publications SS20018

= Take a piece of coat puzzle.

= Move across.

= Lose 1 turn.

= Move back 1.

= Move two times your roll.

= Move ahead 1.

= Move ahead 2.

Game Board

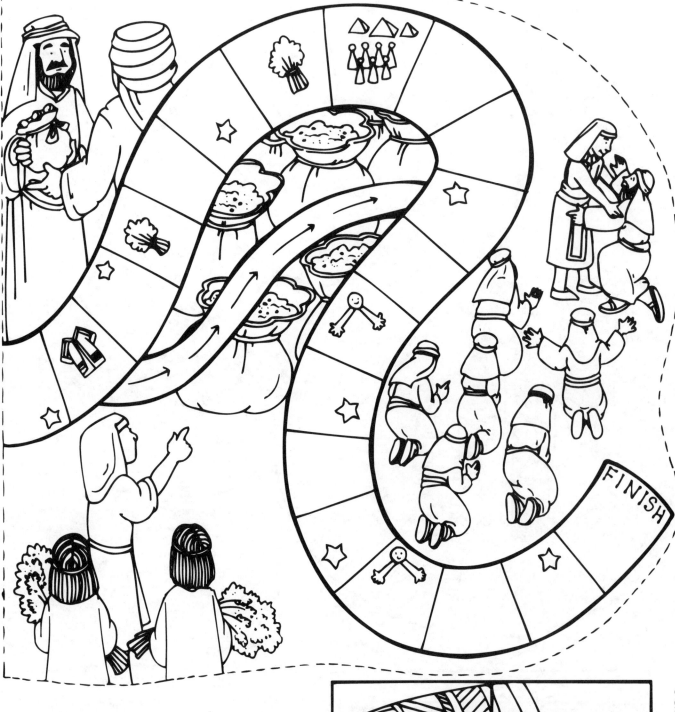

He Is the Vine

Jesus said that He is the vine and we are the branches. (John 15:5) In order to bear fruit in our lives, we need to stay connected to Jesus. We need to remain in Him by studying His Word, praying, worshipping, and obeying His commands. By doing these things, we will show that we are Jesus' disciples, and this is how we can "bear fruit" for Him. You will enjoy watching children share their knowledge of what it means to "bear fruit" as they play this game together.

Materials Needed

- 1 copy of the Bible verse card below
- 1 copy of the labels and cards on page 58
- 2 copies of the bunches of grapes on page 59
- 1 copy of the spinner on page 59
- manila file folder
- 2-quart resealable plastic freezer bag
- clothespin
- scissors
- crayons
- glue
- tagboard
- 40 pennies
- paper fastener

Directions

1. Color, cut out, and mount the game label on the front of the file folder.
2. Color, cut out, and mount the file folder tab label onto the tab of the file folder.
3. Cut out and mount the Bible verse card on the top left-hand side of the inside of the folder.
4. Cut out the directions card and extra fun card. Mount them on tagboard and place them inside the plastic bag.
5. Color and cut out the bunches of grapes. Mount them on the inside of the file folder as shown.
6. Color the spinner, mount it on tagboard, and cut it out.
7. Insert a paper fastener through the center of the spinner. Then insert it through a 5" x 5" inch piece of tagboard. Be sure the spinner spins freely. Draw an arrow on the base of the assembled spinner as shown and place it in the plastic bag along with the pennies.
8. Clip the bag to the folder with the clothespin, or drop it inside the file folder.
9. Model how to play the game from start to finish.

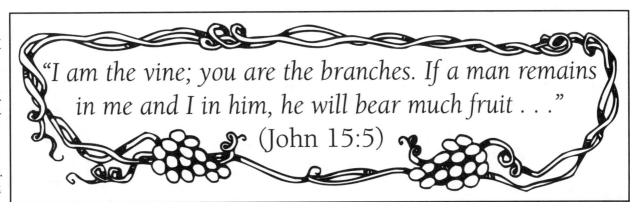

"*I am the vine; you are the branches. If a man remains in me and I in him, he will bear much fruit . . .*"

(John 15:5)

Game Label

He Is the Vine

Extra Fun!

Extra Fun!

Cut ten 3-inch circles from purple or green construction paper to represent grapes. Draw a vine across the top of a sheet of paper with a brown crayon or marker. Write *Jesus* along the length of the vine. Each time you do something for the Lord, paste one of the grapes on the vine. Hang this where you will see it as a reminder to "remain in Him and bear fruit."

Directions Card

He Is the Vine

Number of Players: 2–4

How to Play:

1. Read the Bible verse aloud.
2. Place the stack of pennies in the middle of the game board.
3. All players choose one bunch of grapes. Then decide who will go first.
4. Player One spins the spinner and places the correct number of grapes (pennies) on his or her bunch.
5. If the spinner points to "pruned," the player must remove 2 grapes.
6. Take turns and continue the game until one player has all 10 grapes on a bunch.
7. At the end of the game, work together to list 10 things that show how you "bear fruit" for Jesus.

File Folder Tab

He Is the Vine

Bunches of Grapes

The Birds of the Air

Genesis 1:20–23 gives a detailed account of the fifth day of creation when God created the birds of the air. And God said, " . . . let birds fly above the earth across the expanse of the sky." So God created . . . every winged bird according to its kind . . . God blessed them and said, "Be fruitful and increase in number . . . and let the birds increase on the earth." (Genesis 1:20–22) Numerous kinds of birds are mentioned throughout the Bible in both the Old and New Testaments. Children will sharpen their Bible knowledge skills as they explore this bird matching game together.

Materials Needed

- 1 copy of the Bible verse card below
- 1 copy of the labels and cards on page 61
- 1 copy of the bird and nest patterns on pages 62 and 63
- manila file folder
- 2-quart resealable plastic freezer bag
- clothespin
- scissors
- crayons

Directions

1. Color, cut out, and mount the game label on the front of the file folder.
2. Color, cut out, and mount the file folder tab on the tab of the file folder.
3. Cut out and mount the Bible verse card on the top left-hand side of the inside of the folder.
4. Cut out the directions card and extra fun card. Mount them on tagboard and place them inside the plastic bag.
5. Color and cut out the nests. Mount them on the inside of the file folder as shown.
6. Color the birds, mount the page on tagboard, cut the birds out, and store them in the plastic bag.
7. Clip the bag to the folder with the clothespin, or drop it inside the file folder.
8. Model how to play the game from start to finish.

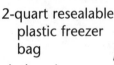
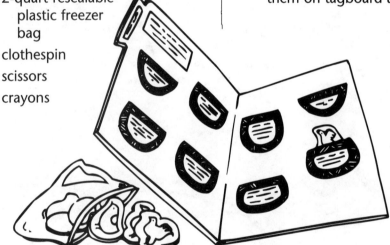

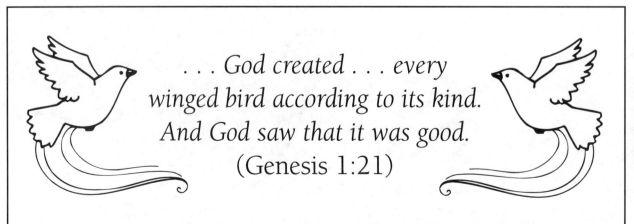

. . . God created . . . every winged bird according to its kind. And God saw that it was good. (Genesis 1:21)

Bible Verse Card

© Shining Star Publications SS20018

Game Label

The Birds of the Air

Extra Fun!

Create a unique bird of your own. Use feathers, construction paper scraps, yarn, modeling dough, glue, scissors, and other collage materials. Be creative and have fun. Then recite Genesis 1:21 aloud as you show friends and family members your new creation.

Directions Card

The Birds of the Air

Number of Players: 1–2

How to Play:

1. Read the Bible verse aloud.
2. Read a Bible verse from one of the nests.
3. Find the matching bird, and set it in the nest.
4. Continue to match all the birds to their nests.

File Folder Tab

The Birds of the Air

Nests

*but those who hope in the Lord will renew their strength. They will soar on wings like **eagles**; they will run and not grow weary . . .* (Isaiah 40:31)

*"O Jerusalem, Jerusalem, . . . how often I have longed to gather your children together, as a **hen** gathers her chicks under her wings, but you were not willing."* (Matthew 23:37)

*The Lord said to Moses, "I have heard the grumbling of the Israelites. Tell them, 'At twilight you will eat meat, and in the morning you will be filled with bread. Then you will know that I am the Lord your God.'" That evening **quail** came and covered the camp . . .* (Exodus 16:11–13)

*After forty days Noah opened the window he had made in the ark and sent out a **raven**, and it kept flying back and forth until the water had dried up from the earth.* (Genesis 8:6–7)

*"Are not five **sparrows** sold for two pennies? Yet not one of them is forgotten by God . . . you are worth more than many sparrows."* (Luke 12:6–7)

*"I tell you the truth," Jesus answered, "this very night, before the **rooster** crows, you will disown me three times."* (Matthew 26:34)

*"'If the offering to the Lord is a burnt offering of birds, he is to offer a dove or a young **pigeon**.'"* (Leviticus 1:14)

*As soon as Jesus was baptized, he went up out of the water. At that moment heaven was opened, and he saw the Spirit of God descending like a **dove** and lighting on him.* (Matthew 3:16)

Birds

Reflections Page

Name _____

My favorite Scripture verse
is _____
_____
because _____
_____
_____

My favorite game is
_____ because
_____
_____
_____
_____

© Shining Star Publications SS20018

64